APR - 2011

LIFE STORIES

ROSA PARKS

Gillian Gosman

PowerKiDS press™

New York

Published in 2011 by The Rosen Publishing Group, Inc.
29 East 21st Street, New York, NY 10010

First Edition

Editor: Jennifer Way
Book Design: Ashley Burrell and Erica Clendening

Photo Credits: Cover (inset) William Philpott/Getty Images; cover (background), pp. 6–7, 12–13, 14–15, 17, 22 (left) Don Cravens/Time & Life Pictures/Getty Images; pp. 4–5 Paul Schutzer/Time & Life Pictures/Getty Images; p. 8 Russell Lee/MPI/Getty Images; pp. 8–9 Hulton Archive/Getty Images; p. 10 FPG/Hulton Archive/ Getty Images; pp. 10–11 Anthony Potter Collection/Getty Images; pp. 13, 16–17, 22 (right) Grey Villet/Time & Life Pictures/Getty Images; pp. 18–19 Rolls Press/Popperfoto/Getty Images; pp. 20–21 Jeff Kowalsky/AFP/ Getty Images.

Library of Congress Cataloging-in-Publication Data

Gosman, Gillian.
 Rosa Parks / by Gillian Gosman. — 1st ed.
    p. cm. — (Life stories)
 ISBN 978-1-4488-2584-4 (library binding) — ISBN 978-1-4488-2757-2 (pbk.) —
ISBN 978-1-4488-2758-9 (6-pack)
 1. Parks, Rosa, 1913-2005—Juvenile literature. 2. African American women—Alabama—Montgomery—Biography—Juvenile literature. 3. African Americans—Alabama—Montgomery—Biography—Juvenile literature. 4. Civil rights workers—Alabama—Montgomery—Biography—Juvenile literature. 5. Montgomery (Ala.)—Biography—Juvenile literature. 6. Montgomery Bus Boycott, Montgomery, Ala., 1955-1956—Juvenile literature. 7. African Americans—Civil rights—Alabama—Montgomery—History—20th century—Juvenile literature. 8. Segregation in transportation—Alabama—Montgomery—History—20th century—Juvenile literature. 9. Montgomery (Ala.)—Race relations—Juvenile literature. I. Title.
 F334.M753P3736 2011
 323.092—dc22
 [B]
                    2010035326

                    36018056648736

Manufactured in the United States of America
CPSIA Compliance Information: Batch #WW11PK: For Further Information contact Rosen Publishing, New York, New York at 1-800-237-9932

CONTENTS

Meet Rosa Parks

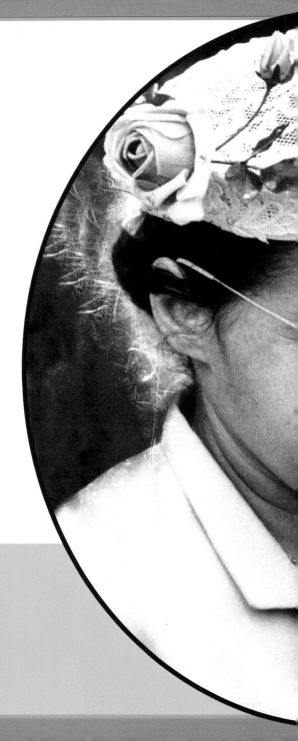

Rosa Parks is often called the mother of the **civil rights movement**. How did one person come to stand for this important cause?

Rosa Parks worked with many civil rights leaders, such as Martin Luther King Jr.

Parks was brave and hardworking. She believed in the **equality** of all people and all races. She put her life on the line to fight for her beliefs.

Young Rosa

Rosa Louise McCauley was born on February 4, 1913, in Tuskegee, Alabama. When she was two, the family moved to Pine Level, Alabama.

Parks worked as a seamstress for many years. A seamstress is a person who sews clothing.

Rosa left high school when her grandmother and mother fell ill. She went back to high school years later and finished when she was 21. In 1932, she married a barber named Raymond Parks and took his name, becoming Rosa Parks.

LIFE IN A SEGREGATED AMERICA

Rosa Parks lived during the time of **segregation**. Whites and blacks went to different schools. They even had to sit in different parts of buses. There was fear and hate between the races. Sometimes there was **violence**.

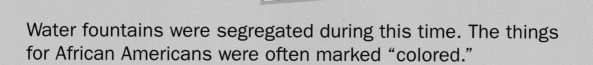

Water fountains were segregated during this time. The things for African Americans were often marked "colored."

This man is standing in front of a store at which only white people were allowed to shop.

Parks and many others wanted to end segregation. The actions that these **activists** took were called the civil rights movement. They used nonviolent **resistance**, including **sit-ins** and **boycotts**.

The Parkses' Politics

Raymond and Rosa Parks spoke out against unfair treatment and gave their time to different causes. They studied nonviolent resistance. They took part in workshops, or classes, on how to have a peaceful **protest**.

These NAACP members are protesting a club that refused to serve African Americans.

The NAACP has chapters all over the United States. This is an NAACP office from the late 1940s.

Raymond and Rosa were members of the National Association for the Advancement of Colored People, or the NAACP. Rosa was the **secretary** and youth leader for the Montgomery chapter.

PLANNING A PROTEST

The civil rights activists of Montgomery wanted to lead a boycott of the city's segregated bus lines. The boycott would cause the city to lose money. If the city lost enough money, it might change its unfair law.

Here is Parks (center) at a meeting led by Martin Luther King Jr. (left).

Many people who took part in the bus boycott walked instead of taking the bus.

Civil rights leaders wanted someone to be the face of the boycott. They wanted someone serious and smart, like Rosa Parks.

Breaking the Law!

On December 1, 1955, Rosa Parks boarded a Montgomery bus. She had just finished a long day of work. On her bus ride home, Parks refused to give her seat to a white rider.

This picture shows Parks (far right) riding a Montgomery bus after the boycott ended.

The bus driver ordered the black riders to give up their seats to make room for more white riders. Parks refused. She was **arrested** for breaking Alabama's segregation law.

THE MONTGOMERY BUS BOYCOTT

After her arrest, Rosa Parks was taken to the police station and charged with breaking Alabama's segregation law. That night, civil rights activists, led by Martin Luther King Jr., met to plan the bus boycott.

Montgomery's buses were nearly empty during the boycott. ↑

The Montgomery bus boycott lasted 381 days. During that time, many boycotters walked to work, even when it rained.

The bus boycott began four days later. Boycotters walked and carpooled instead of taking the bus. After 381 days, a court decided that Montgomery's segregated buses were illegal.

A Great First Step

The Montgomery bus boycott was an important moment in the civil rights movement. Rosa Parks helped get it started.

The 1960s brought new civil rights laws. Here President Lyndon B. Johnson (seated) signs the Civil Rights Act of 1968 into law.

During the boycott, civil rights activists were treated with fear and hate. In the end, the boycott showed whites that the activists were serious. It showed the activists that if they worked together, they could change unfair laws.

Life After the Boycott

After the boycott, the Parks family moved to Detroit, Michigan. Rosa got a job in the office of African-American congressman John Conyers Jr. She worked for him from 1965 until 1988.

Parks was given a Congressional Gold Medal in 1999 to honor her work for civil rights.

In the 1980s, Parks created a number of groups and **scholarships** for young people. She wrote the story of her life. She gave many public speeches, too. Rosa Parks died on October 24, 2005. She was 92 years old.

TIMELINE

February 4, 1913

Rosa Louise McCauley is born in Tuskegee, Alabama.

December 1, 1955

Parks refuses to give up her bus seat and is arrested.

December 5, 1955

The Montgomery bus boycott begins.

October 24, 2005

Rosa Parks dies.

1965

Parks begins working in Congressman John Conyers's office in Detroit.

December 20, 1956

The Montgomery bus boycott ends.

Glossary

activists (AK-tih-vists) People who take action for what they believe is right.

arrested (uh-REST-ed) Stopped a person who is thought to have committed a crime.

boycotts (BOY-kots) Refusals to deal with people, nations, or businesses.

civil rights movement (SIH-vul RYTS MOOV-mint) People and groups working together to win freedom and equality for all.

equality (ih-KWAH-luh-tee) Being equal.

protest (PROH-test) An act of disagreement.

resistance (rih-ZIS-tens) A strong stand taken against something.

scholarships (SKAH-lur-ships) Money given to people to pay for school.

secretary (SEK-ruh-ter-ee) The person who keeps the records for a group.

segregation (seh-grih-GAY-shun) The act of keeping people of one race, sex, or social class away from others.

sit-ins (SIT-inz) Acts of protest at which generally groups of black people refuse to move out of a white-only part of a public place.

violence (VY-lens) Strong force used to hurt someone or something.

Index

Web Sites

Due to the changing nature of Internet links, PowerKids Press has developed an online list of Web sites related to the subject of this book. This site is updated regularly. Please use this link to access the list:
www.powerkidslinks.com/life/rparks/